# THE FIRST TRANSATLANTIC FLIGHT

## Mike Rosen

Illustrated by Richard Scollins

The Bookwright Press
New York • 1989

# Great Journeys

**The Conquest of Everest**
**The First Men on the Moon**
**The First Transatlantic Flight**
**The First Voyage Around the World**
**The Race to the South Pole**
**The Travels of Marco Polo**
**The Voyage of Columbus**
**The Voyage of the Beagle**

*Frontispiece* Captain John Alcock and Lieutenant Arthur Whitten Brown, who, in their Vickers Vimy, made the first transatlantic flight in 1919.

*Cover* The Vickers Vimy used by John Alcock and Arthur Whitten Brown was a bomber, which had been specially converted for the transatlantic flight. This painting shows the Vimy in the middle of its crossing, passing over the rough seas of the Atlantic ocean.

First published in the
United States in 1989 by
The Bookwright Press
387 Park Avenue South
New York, NY 10016

First published in 1989 by
Wayland (Publishers) Limited
61 Western Road, Hove
East Sussex, BN3 1JD, England

© Copyright 1989 Wayland (Publishers) Limited

Typeset by Lizzie George, Wayland
Printed in Italy by G. Canale & C.S.p.A., Turin

**Library of Congress Cataloging-in-Publication Data**
Rosen, Mike.
　The first transatlantic flight / by Mike Rosen.
　　p. cm.—(Great journeys)
　Bibliography: p.
　Includes index.
　Summary: Describes the first flight over the Atlantic from Canada to Great Britain made in 1919 by John Alcock and Arthur Whitten Brown and the first solo flight from New York to Paris made in 1927 by Charles Lindbergh.
　　ISBN 0-531-18303-3
　　1. Transatlantic flights—Juvenile literature. 2. Alcock, John, Sir, 1892–1919—Juvenile literature. 3. Brown, Arthur Whitten, Sir, 1886–1948—Juvenile literature. 4. Lindbergh, Charles A. (Charles Augustus), 1902–1974—Juvenile literature. [1. Transatlantic flights. 2. Alcock, John, Sir, 1892–1919. 3. Brown, Arthur Whitten, Sir, 1886–1948. 4. Lindbergh, Charles A. (Charles Augustus), 1902–1974.] I. Title. II. Series.
TL531.R67 1990
629.13'09111—dc 19　　　　　　　　　　　　89-31199
　　　　　　　　　　　　　　　　　　　　　CIP
　　　　　　　　　　　　　　　　　　　　　AC

# Contents

1. Into the Sky — 4
2. Early Flight 1908-1919 — 6
3. Atlantic Challenge — 8
4. Preparations in Britain — 10
5. Newfoundland — 12
6. A Problem Halved — 14
7. The Race Against Time — 16
8. Ready for Takeoff — 18
9. Across the Atlantic — 20
10. Crash Landing — 22
11. New Adventures — 24
12. Charles Lindbergh — 26
13. Flying the Atlantic — 28

Glossary — 30
Finding Out More — 31
Index — 32

# Into the Sky

On June 14, 1919, two pilots, John Alcock and Arthur Whitten Brown, took off in an attempt to fly non-stop across the Atlantic Ocean from Canada to Britain. The dangers were many. Besides the strain on pilot and airplane during such a long flight, there was the added problem of the Atlantic weather.

The North Atlantic Ocean is nearly 3,000 km (1,800 mi) wide at its narrowest point – in places it is deeper than Mount Everest is high. Fierce storms produce waves 30 m (100 ft) tall and gale force winds of up to 140 km an hour (90 mph). Massive banks of clouds may tower to an altitude of many thousands of feet above sea level. In these clouds a pilot could lose all sense of direction and fly disastrously off course. At higher altitudes, freezing fog could form ice on an airplane's wings, engine and control cables, making the aircraft uncontrollable. These were the dangers Alcock and Brown set out to conquer in their transatlantic flight.

*Below* In 1903 Wilbur and Orville Wright, in their Wright Flyer I, made the first powered flight at Kitty Hawk in North Carolina.

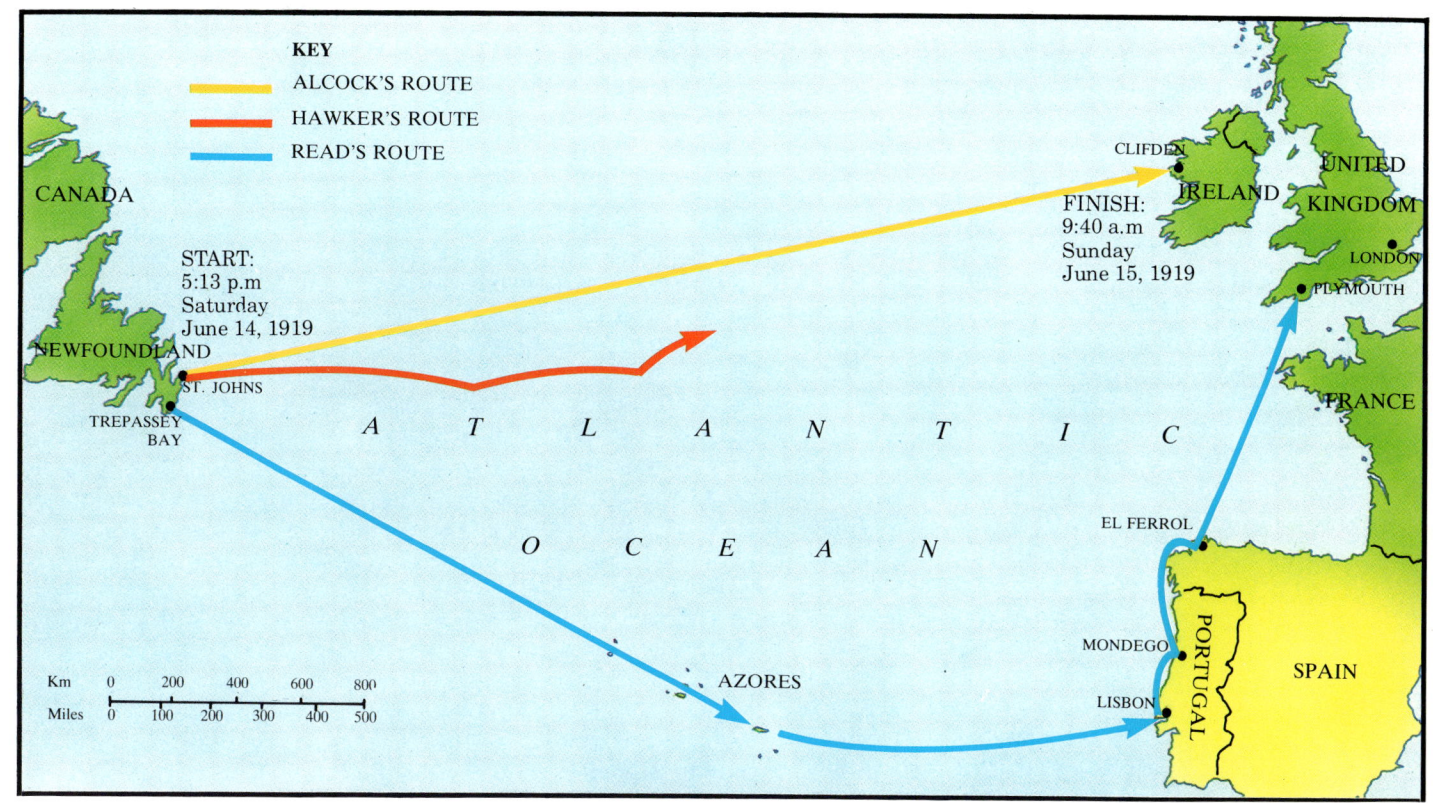

Amazingly, Alcock and Brown's attempt came just sixteen years after the Wright brothers had first shown that controlled powered flight was possible. On December 17, 1903, six men had celebrated as Orville Wright flew the *Flyer* a distance of 40 m (130 ft), remaining airborne for 12 seconds. One of the six men was Wilbur Wright, Orville's brother, who later that day made a flight of 59 seconds – flying just under 285 m (900 ft).

Orville and Wilbur Wright had spent four years developing their airplane. It was based on their many experiments with gliders. The vital element in its design was their discovery of "wing warping." Watching the flight of buzzards near their home in Dayton, Ohio, the Wrights saw how birds controlled their stability when gliding. The buzzards they studied twisted the ends of their wings slightly, changing their angle and altering the force of the air flowing over them. When the Wrights applied this principle to one of their gliders it gave them greatly improved control.

After the historic flight of 1903, the Wright brothers spent several years improving their airplane. A longer body gave the airplane more stability in flight, while new engines and more efficient propellers gave greater speed and power. By 1908, Orville was performing test flights, which included turns and figures of eight, for the U.S. Army. Wilbur was in France, demonstrating the latest Wright *Flyer*.

**Above** *This map shows the different routes across the Atlantic taken by three of the competitors in the Transatlantic Race.*

# Early Flight 1908-1919

After Wilbur Wright's visit to France in 1908, European airplane design improved greatly. At Farnborough in Britain, the British Army was trying to manufacture a practical airplane with the help of Samuel F. Cody. Cody was an American. At different times he had been a cowboy, a rodeo rider, and a traveling showman. His pioneer spirit was well suited to the dangers of early flight.

The design of Cody's airplane was based on the principles discovered by the Wrights. On October 16, 1908, Cody was testing his machine on the ground, getting the feel of some of the changes that had been made. As the machine was running down a slope, it unexpectedly took off. Cody, taken by surprise, was unable to bring it down again. Seeing a clump of trees ahead, he decided it would be safer to fly over them. Finally, while turning in an attempt to land, he crashed. Cody was unhurt. By a mixture of mistakes and good luck, Cody had just made the first recorded flight in Britain, a distance of about 460 m (1,500 ft).

Cody's later attempts to fly his airplane were dogged by bad luck. Finally, at an official trial on January 20, 1909, the front of his airplane broke shortly after takeoff. Cody escaped unhurt but the Army had run out of patience. In April 1909 the War Office stopped the development of Cody's airplane because it was becoming too expensive.

Another reason for stopping Cody's work was that other airplanes that flew successfully were being built. On July 25, 1909, came the exciting news that Louis Blériot had successfully flown from France across the English Channel. Blériot's machine was a monoplane; it had only one set of wings instead of the two used in the design of the biplane. Another technical advance was introduced by Henri Farman of France.

**Above** The American aviator Samuel F. Cody attempted to design an airplane for practical commercial production.

**Far right** The Vickers Vimy, in which Alcock and Brown made the first non-stop transatlantic flight.

Instead of twisting the whole wing, as the Wright design did, Farman had set movable flaps called ailerons into the outer rear corner of each wing. These proved to be a much simpler way of controlling the aircraft.

By 1914 the airplane was taking the form we know today. The outbreak of World War I, forced governments to develop new, more efficient machines for war in the air. By the end of the war in 1918, airplanes could fly long distances at speeds five times faster than the first Wright *Flyer*. Among these airplanes was the Vickers Vimy bomber, the machine Alcock and Brown would use in their attempt to fly the Atlantic non-stop.

**Right** *In 1909, Louis Blériot flew alone across the channel.*

# Atlantic Challenge

**Left** *Aviation quickly became more and more popular. This picture shows a flyby at Reims in France in 1909.*

**Above** *Captain John Alcock*

**Below** *Lieutenant Arthur Whitten Brown*

The challenge of flying the Atlantic had fascinated pilots since Blériot had flown over the English Channel in 1909. Most experts thought it impossible. In 1913, a British newspaper, the *Daily Mail*, offered a prize of £10,000 ($50,000) for the first team to complete a non-stop crossing of the Atlantic. The owner of the *Daily Mail*, Lord Alfred Northcliffe, wanted to encourage the development of flight. But before anyone could attempt the challenge, World War I broke out, in August 1914.

Four years later, the pilots and aircraft makers renewed their interest in the *Daily Mail* challenge. Four British companies finally competed – Handley Page, Martinsyde, Sopwith and Vickers. Vickers chose John Alcock as pilot.

Born in Manchester in 1892, John Alcock was a trained engineer. In 1910 he was engaged as a mechanic at Brooklands. Brooklands was one of Europe's most famous motor-racing tracks. In 1910 many airplane designers worked there, developing their machines. Alcock worked as mechanic to a French pilot, Ducrocq, who taught him to fly.

Alcock loved flying. He entered every air race he could and soon attracted attention with a victory at Hendon in Britain. Eventually, the Sunbeam company gave him a job as a test pilot. Although the job was dangerous, it gave Alcock vital flying experience. He became an expert at handling airplanes in difficult conditions, flying them to the limits of their capabilities. As a test pilot, part of his job was to suggest improvements to the machines he flew. Using his engineer's training, Alcock learned much about how to keep an airplane flying reliably.

During World War I, John Alcock joined the Royal Naval Air Service. Toward the end of the war he was shot down over Turkey and taken prisoner. While imprisoned, he planned how he would fly across the Atlantic after the war was over. When he was released, Alcock went to meet the staff of Vickers. There he was shown a Vickers Vimy being prepared for the *Daily Mail* prize. Vickers knew of Alcock's flying skills and knowledge of airplanes. Impressed by his ideas about flying the Atlantic, Vickers gave Alcock the job he had dreamed about in prison.

The search began for a navigator. In those days airplanes had no modern pathfinding equipment. Without a navigator, Alcock would never be able to find his way across the ocean. One day Arthur Whitten Brown walked into Vickers' offices, looking for work as an engineer. He started talking about the *Daily Mail* prize, and the problem was solved. Whitten Brown had been shot down over France during the war and had been taken prisoner. To ease the boredom of prison life he had taught himself the skills of navigation. He had even worked out a route for crossing the Atlantic. The Vickers team was now complete.

*Below* This cartoon was published in 1913 and shows Britain's growing interest in aviation. It depicts Britannia putting on "The Wings of Victory."

# Preparations in Britain

The Vickers Vimy was one of the largest planes available. It had been designed as a bomber. Powered by two Rolls Royce Eagle VIII engines, it could fly at around 175 km per hour (100 mph). During World War I these airplanes had shown their capacity for long-distance flight.

The Vimy that Alcock and Brown were to use was being altered to suit their journey. The bomb racks and the gunner's cockpit were removed and extra fuel tanks were fitted. The Vimy would need every bit of fuel it could carry. One of the fuel tanks was designed to be used – when empty – as a lifeboat, should Alcock and Brown be forced to land in the water. A radio was fitted in the cockpit so that the pilots could keep in contact with the world during their journey. The engines were built with great care because they would have to work perfectly for many hours.

While the Vimy was being constructed, Alcock and Brown planned their route. Like all the entrants for the *Daily Mail* prize, they knew they would have to travel from west to east across the Atlantic. If they did not fly in this direction, they would be flying against the wind all the way. This would increase the amount of fuel used, and reduce their air speed. They would probably never make it. It was not until 1928 that a successful crossing was made from east to west.

Flying the Atlantic from west to east meant starting from North America. The shortest distance lay between the Canadian territory of Newfoundland and the west coast of Ireland. This route was 3,000 km (1,800 mi) and far from the main shipping lanes. If they had serious problems, Alcock and Brown were unlikely to be near help.

**Right** *Alcock and Brown in their flying suits.*

**Below** *The Vimy was carefully tested before it was taken apart and packed into crates for its journey to Newfoundland by freighter.*

Finally, the Vimy was complete. Alcock took it for a test flight. It handled beautifully. Although the test was done without a full fuel load, Alcock was convinced that the extra weight would not be a problem. He and Brown were full of confidence.

Their flying equipment arrived. In addition to Brown's navigational instruments, there were special flying clothes. Alcock had a jacket with an inflatable tube around the waist – a sort of simple lifejacket. Brown had an electrically heated vest. This was fixed to wires that took the electric current down to a pair of heated insoles in his flying boots.

When all the preparations were complete, the Vimy was taken apart and packed into sturdy wooden crates. There was a crate for the fuselage, another for the engines, and two for the wings. Along with other equipment, they were loaded onto a freighter for the journey to Newfoundland. Alcock and Brown went by ship and rail ahead of the Vimy.

# Newfoundland

**Left** *Newfoundland, the starting place of the first transatlantic flight.*

Alcock and Brown arrived in St. John's, Newfoundland in Canada, late in the evening of May 13, 1919. They took rooms at the Cochrane Hotel. At breakfast the next morning they were greeted by most of their rivals. There were four groups competing for the *Daily Mail* prize. The Sopwith pilot was Harry Hawker, a well-known test pilot. Martinsyde had Frederick Raynham, who in 1911 had taught Harry Hawker to fly. Finally there was the Handley Page team, led by Admiral Kerr. Each pilot had a navigator, and a crew of mechanics. The Cochrane Hotel was the base for the Sopwith and Martinsyde teams. The Handley Page team was staying several miles away.

Although there was fierce rivalry among the pilots to be first across the Atlantic, they were also friends. In the evenings they ate and talked together at the Cochrane Hotel. Raynham, the Martinsyde pilot, had known John Alcock at Brooklands motor-racing track before the war. Now, thrown together, far from home, the pilots were glad to be able to discuss their problems with friends.

Both Raynham, the Martinsyde pilot, and Hawker, the Sopwith pilot, were ready to take off when Alcock and Brown arrived. The Handley Page aircraft was being assembled. With their airplane still on the way from Britain, it looked as if Alcock and Brown

would be too late to enter the race. But in fact, the weather was helping them. Fierce spring storms were battering Newfoundland daily, and even test flights were impossible. Every day Raynham and Hawker went to the weather station for forecasts. Eventually the pilots agreed to inform each other of any decision to take off.

Alcock and Brown's most immediate need was for an airfield. Newfoundland did not have an airdrome, and there was a shortage of flat land. The Sopwith and Martinsyde teams had already taken the best sites. Admiral Kerr's Handley Page team had to demolish three houses and clear an enormous field of boulders before they could assemble their plane!

Alcock toured the island by car, desperately searching for a suitable field. Fully loaded, the Vimy would need at least 500 m (1,640 ft) of smooth ground for takeoff. The only suitable fields were already planted with crops.

On the May 17 came news that increased the urgency of their search. An American flying boat had just reached the mid-Atlantic islands of the Azores. It was the last of four flying boats that had left Newfoundland the evening before. Although the flight was not an attempt to win the *Daily Mail* prize, it would make any other crossing of the Atlantic seem less impressive.

**Below** *Alcock and Brown had great difficulty in finding a suitable location for their takeoff. They searched the area by car, looking for a place they could adapt to form an airfield.*

# A Problem Halved

May 18 was a fine day, the first for many weeks. Both Hawker and Raynham decided it was time to go. The Vimy had still not arrived. Frustrated, Alcock and Brown continued their search for a suitable field. Meanwhile, the Sopwith and the Martinsyde airplanes were being fueled. The weather reports said nothing to make Hawker or Raynham change their plans. That afternoon Hawker opened his airplane's throttle and headed down the bumpy field. After 300 m (1,000 ft) his plane left the ground – a few minutes later it was gone.

Over at Quidi Vidi, Raynham's airfield, the Martinsyde aircraft was almost ready. Although Hawker had already left, Raynham was not worried. The Martinsyde was ten miles an hour faster than the Sopwith – he could give Hawker a start and still be first to Britain. When his plane was finally ready, Raynham and his navigator, Fairfax Morgan, climbed aboard. Watched by a cheering crowd, Raynham began his takeoff run. Unluckily, the wind was blowing from the side. When the Martinsyde hit a bump it

**Below** *Raynham, the pilot for the Martinsyde team, crashed as he attempted to take off from his airfield, which was called Quidi Vidi. Both he and his navigator were injured and his plane was damaged beyond repair.*

was lifted into the air too early. Raynham tried to keep his plane flying, but it came down heavily, breaking the landing wheels. One of its wing-tips touched the ground and the nose of the plane dug into the earth as the stunned crowd watched in silence.

When Alcock and Brown returned to the Cochrane Hotel that evening they heard the news. Raynham was there with his head bandaged. Morgan was in the hospital. Raynham offered Alcock and Brown the use of his airfield at Quidi Vidi. With his machine smashed, his navigator injured, and Hawker halfway to Britain, Raynham had lost interest in the Atlantic flight.

All the pilots waited anxiously for news of Hawker's arrival in Britain, but none came. Finally they knew Hawker must have been forced down over the ocean. With no news, they could only assume that Hawker had not been rescued. It was a sad reminder of the dangers they all faced in their efforts to fly the Atlantic.

Alcock and Brown were glad to have an airfield at last. On May 26 the crates containing the Vimy finally arrived. To get them to the airfield at Quidi Vidi took most of the day. On Newfoundland's narrow, twisting lanes, transporting the wagon, which was 20 m (60 ft) long, proved difficult. The walls of one bridge had to be knocked down to get it through. When they got to Quidi Vidi they found that the hangar was too small to build the Vimy inside. A set of canvas screens was put up to provide shelter. Alcock and Brown were back in the race.

# The Race Against Time

Then good news arrived. Hawker and his navigator were safe. The Sopwith's engine had overheated, and they had been forced to land in the ocean. For two hours they had searched for a ship to land next to. News of the rescue could not be given until they reached Scotland because the ship that rescued them had no radio. Relieved that his friends were safe, Alcock asked for details of why the Sopwith's engine had failed. The answer was that dirt in the water had blocked the engine's cooling system causing it to lose power. Alcock decided that all the Vimy's cooling water should be filtered carefully before they filled the radiators. Such attention to detail could save their lives.

Work on rebuilding the Vimy was delayed by the weather. Even when it was not raining, the biting cold made work outside difficult. The mechanics found it hard to concentrate and had problems handling the tools and parts

**Below** *The Vimy was reassembled in the open air, and bad weather conditions made the work slow and difficult. This picture shows the mechanics working on one of the wings.*

when their fingers were frozen by the wind. They often had to rest, for the safety of the pilots depended on how well the mechanics did their job. Despite the problems, the Vimy was put together by the mechanics in only two weeks.

While the Vimy was being assembled, Alcock and Brown were still trying to find a suitable airfield. Quidi Vidi was fine for smaller planes and for test flights, but the Vimy could not take off there with a full load of fuel. Desperate, they finally found exactly what they needed. It was a 300 m (1,000 ft) field with another long stretch of open land beyond. It took them three days to get the airfield ready; trees and boulders had to be moved and a ditch filled in. They named it Lester's Field. Just as they had finished, the Handley Page flew overhead. Alcock and Brown were afraid it was on its way to cross the Atlantic. They were pleased when it turned back, but they knew they had little time left.

The Vimy was flown from Quidi Vidi to the new airfield. It flew perfectly, but there was a problem with the fuel. Somehow it had become full of a gummy substance, and there was a danger it could damage the engines. Raynham gave them what was left of his fuel, and they used this until more could arrive from Britain.

By June 13 they had new fuel and the weather was perfect. Mechanics began to fuel the Vimy. The fuel was filtered twice before it was put into the tanks. It was slow work. Then in mid-afternoon, when the tanks were nearly full, part of the landing gear collapsed. The fuel tanks had to be emptied again, and the mechanics worked late into the night to repair the damage.

**Above** *Slowly the airplane took shape. Rebuilding the Vimy was like fitting together the pieces of a giant jigsaw puzzle.*

17

# Ready for Takeoff

The weather was still fine the next morning, though strong winds were gusting across Lester's Field. A large crowd had arrived to watch Alcock and Brown leave. The flyers arrived early and checked over the airplane. Official badges were attached to the fuselage to prove, should it be successful, that it was the same machine that had left Newfoundland. Late in the morning the plane was pushed across the field so that its takeoff run would face into the wind. After lunch, the wind was still gusting strongly. Despite this, Alcock and Brown decided it was time to leave.

The two men climbed into the cockpit. Brown made sure that all his navigation equipment was on board. Alcock calmly checked that the gauges and instruments were working. A row of men took position in front of each wing, ready to hold the Vimy back while Alcock tested the engines. For a few moments Alcock sat silent. Then he looked at Brown, and gave the order for the engines to be started. With a healthy roar

**Above** *After Alcock and Brown had thoroughly checked it, the Vimy was ready for takeoff.*

**Below** *The plane had to be turned and pushed into position by the mechanics.*

**Above** *The crowds that had gathered to watch the takeoff waved as the Vimy pulled above the trees.*

they burst into life. Clouds of blue smoke from the exhaust disappeared as the engines settled to a steady beat.

Waving to the watching crowd, Alcock gave the signal for the wings to be released. The men holding them let go together, and the Vimy began its run. Slowly it accelerated, bumping over the rough surface of Lester's Field. At the last possible moment, Alcock pulled back on the control stick. Reluctantly, the overloaded Vimy struggled into the air. Clearing a row of trees with only a few yards to spare, it disappeared over the crest of a hill. Minutes later, the anxious crowd cheered as the Vimy came back into sight, climbing toward the Atlantic.

In the Vimy, Brown noticed that Alcock was wet with nervous sweat. At that moment the radio went dead; the propeller that powered its generator had broken off. They had no way of calling for help should they need it.

Now that they had survived the takeoff, it was time for Brown to set their course. The first step was to note from which point of the compass the sun was shining. Brown used his sextant to work out the angle between the position of the sun and the horizon. With the help of navigation tables, Brown could now work out the sun's position, relative to the Earth for that date and time. With all this information Brown could finally plot their position on his chart of the Atlantic. A series of such positional readings allowed him to plot their course.

# Across the Atlantic

No sooner had Brown set their course than things began to go wrong. Fog covered the ocean, and a haze of cloud hid the sun. They now had no way of checking their position. Then the exhaust pipe on the right-hand engine began to work loose. Gradually the pipe split along its length, glowing red-hot as the exhaust gases escaped. Finally it tore off. The noise from the unsilenced exhaust was ear shattering. Flames spat from the engine outlet, only a few feet away from the cockpit. Luckily the canvas covering of the wings did not catch fire.

Gritting their teeth against the awful noise, Alcock and Brown flew on. Brown got out the sandwiches and hot coffee. Alcock ate and drank with one hand, never letting go of the controls. After supper, they climbed above the clouds so that Brown could take readings of their position from the stars. At 2,000 m (6,600 ft) above sea level, the air was bitterly cold. Brown's fingers ached as he calculated. They were halfway to Ireland, having flown 1,360 km (800 mi) in eight hours.

A pale moon lit the surface of the clouds beneath them. It

***Below*** *The exhaust pipe on the right-hand engine of the Vimy split soon after takeoff. This caused the flight to be not only uncomfortably noisy but also highly dangerous as flames spat freely out of the engine.*

cast strange shadows and changed the appearance of the clouds. Above them, the stars glimmered. As the night wore on, and the engines droned steadily, Alcock and Brown fought to stay awake.

Suddenly they were in thick cloud. Alcock, tired and unable to see through the mist, lost control of the Vimy. In fierce winds the plane was thrown in all directions. The instruments were useless and the speed indicator jammed. Then they were falling. Spinning out of control, the Vimy fell toward the ocean. For 1,000 m (3,000 ft) they fell in near silence. They heard only the quiet note of the engines idling, and the rush of air past the wings. Then they could hear the roar of the waves below. Alcock and Brown prepared themselves for the crash.

Only 30 m (100 ft) from disaster the cloud broke. His vision restored, Alcock knew he had to act fast. The Vimy was upside down, spinning toward the waves. All the years he had spent testing airplanes to their limits helped Alcock in that moment. Opening the throttles, he desperately wrestled with the control lever. The engines roared and the Vimy rolled over. Shuddering from the strain, the Vimy climbed away from the threatening ocean.

**Above** *At one point Alcock lost control of the plane and it went into a spin, falling toward the water. Only his great flying experience saved them from crashing into the ocean.*

# Crash Landing

After their narrow escape Alcock and Brown decided to fly above the clouds. As they flew higher the air got colder. Rain turned to snow, and ice began to cover the wings. A vital fuel-pressure gauge became impossible to read. Brown had to leave his seat, hang over the edge of the cockpit holding a wing strut and wipe the gauge clean. The air outside the cockpit was freezing, and the force of the wind almost blew him away.

Once above the clouds, at a height of 3,500 m (11,500 ft) Brown checked their position. They were only 130 km (80 mi) from Ireland. Then the right-hand engine began to misfire.

**Right** *Clifden in Connemara, Southern Ireland.*

Ice was blocking the air intake. Without air the engine was choking, unable to function properly. Alcock shut it down and began to glide. They would not be able to reach Ireland on one engine, but Alcock was sure that at a lower altitude the ice would melt, and the engine could be restarted. At 200 m (650 ft) above the sea, Alcock started the engine. Instantly, it burst into life.

Within 45 minutes they crossed the coast of Ireland. Now they only had to find a place to land. Next to a military camp in Clifden, they saw a large green field. It looked ideal. As they came closer they could see people in the field waving. Cheerfully, Alcock waved back. In fact the people were trying to warn Alcock not to land there because the field was a peat bog. When the Vimy touched down the surface gave way.

The worried crowd rushed toward the crashed Vimy, but Alcock and Brown got out unhurt. Their flight had taken them 16 hours and 28 minutes. At first, nobody would believe that they had just flown across the Atlantic, but messages were sent to London, announcing Alcock and Brown's safe arrival. These messages were followed by the return of the pilots. They traveled by train, and crowds greeted them at many of the major railroad stations on their journey. In London, they were driven to a reception held in their honor, where they received the *Daily Mail*'s prize. They were later knighted at Buckingham Palace.

After the celebrations, Alcock and Brown went back to their jobs. Although he never flew again, Brown worked in the aircraft industry until his death in 1948. Alcock was killed in a flying accident in December 1919.

*Left* Alcock and Brown at the wireless station in Clifden, shortly after their landing.

*Above* When they arrived in London, the two pilots were greeted with great enthusiasm.

*Far left* Their landing was not particularly graceful and the Vimy ended up nose first in a bog.

# New Adventures

Alcock and Brown's flight began a new era in aviation. Later the same year, in December 1919, four Australian pilots took off in another Vickers Vimy. Their aim was to fly the 12,000 km (7,000 mi) from London to Australia. Unlike Alcock and Brown's flight, this was not a non-stop attempt because the distance was too great.

Led by Ross Smith, the Australian team faced many difficulties. Forced to land by strong winds over what is now called Iraq, they found themselves in a sandstorm. Fierce winds threatened to blow the Vimy over, and fifty soldiers from a nearby camp had to help hold it down. Everywhere they went, the landing strips were dangerous. In Singapore the runway was too short and another airfield was covered with tree stumps; Ross Smith just managed to dodge between them.

Ross Smith and his team reached Australia in 28 days. The following year, 1920, two pilots flew from London to South Africa. They started from London in a Vickers Vimy, which was by now the preferred airplane for long-distance flights. A forced landing in the Sahara wrecked the plane, but once they had been rescued, the two pilots continued their attempt in a second Vimy. This too was wrecked in a crash and they finally reached Cape Town 45 days after leaving London – in their third plane.

Everywhere, pilots and aircraft-makers were thinking of new long-distance flights that could be made. In 1924 a team of U.S. Army Air Force planes flew around the world. They made 72 stops during their 175-day journey. With all the resources of a military

**Above** *The Australian team that won the Great Air Race from London to Darwin in 1919.*

**Right** *Charles Kingsford-Smith*

**Far Right** *Amy Johnson*

organization, the pilots had few problems.

The explorer Richard Byrd flew from Norway to the North Pole and back in 1926. Three years later, in 1929, Byrd flew over the South Pole. A year earlier, 1928, three German pilots made the first crossing of the Atlantic from east to west, a feat believed impossible only nine years earlier.

Also in 1928, Charles Kingsford-Smith and his crew flew across the Pacific from California to Australia. This was the most dangerous long-distance flight of all. The first leg of the flight, from San Francisco to Hawaii, required perfect navigation. Even a tiny mistake could leave the plane lost above the vast Pacific Ocean. Despite these dangers, and although they flew through violent storms, Kingsford-Smith's team made the flight in only 11 days.

By the mid-1920s many long-distance passenger routes had been established. Travelers flew all over the world from London and other European cities. Imperial Airways, flying from Croydon Airport in Britain, ran regular flights to India, Australia, and Africa. Within the United States, air travel was popular too. As air travel increased, the excitement caused by long-distance flights lessened. Then on May 20, 1927, the world was gripped by startling news. A young American pilot, Charles Lindbergh, had left New York to fly to Paris on his own. No one had ever flown such a distance across an ocean without a crew to help.

**Above** *Richard Byrd*

**Below** *This map shows the routes taken by some of the other long-distance aviators of the time.*

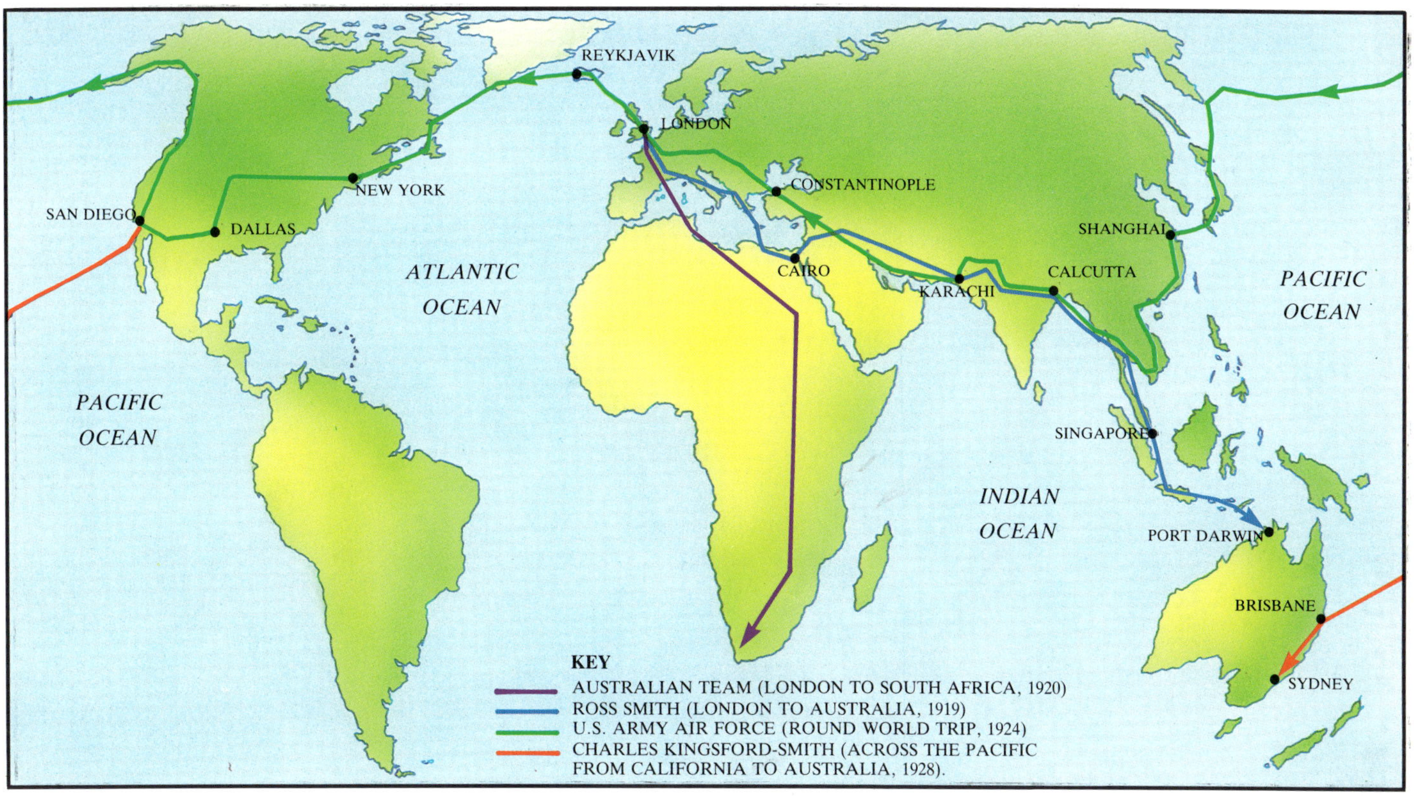

**KEY**
AUSTRALIAN TEAM (LONDON TO SOUTH AFRICA, 1920)
ROSS SMITH (LONDON TO AUSTRALIA, 1919)
U.S. ARMY AIR FORCE (ROUND WORLD TRIP, 1924)
CHARLES KINGSFORD-SMITH (ACROSS THE PACIFIC FROM CALIFORNIA TO AUSTRALIA, 1928).

# Charles Lindbergh

Charles Lindbergh's flying career had been full of danger. He had worked as a stuntman, or barnstormer, in a flying circus. The most spectacular parts of a barnstorming display were when men and women made parachute jumps, or stood on the wings of speeding aircraft during exhibitions of aerobatics.

In 1922 Lindbergh got a job with an airmail company. However bad the weather, he had to fly, for the letters could not be delayed. On one occasion, thick cloud covered the ground. Searching for a place to land, Lindbergh realized he was running out of fuel. He parachuted out and landed safely. The next day he collected the letters from the wrecked plane and delivered them in a new machine. The mail was still on time.

Large crowds came to see Lindbergh take off from New York. Although heavily loaded, Lindbergh's plane, the *Spirit of St. Louis*, handled well and the first part of the flight went smoothly. As the hours passed Lindbergh's greatest enemy became his own tiredness. His straining eyes saw ghostly images, he imagined voices talking to him in the cockpit.

**Above** Mechanics posing for a photograph with Lindbergh's plane, The Spirit of St. Louis.

**Above right** Charles Lindbergh, the first person to fly alone across the Atlantic.

**Below right** Mrs. Victor Bruce, the British aviator who flew alone around the world in 1930.

Halfway across the ocean his eyes began to close as desperately he fought to remain awake. Leaning out of the cockpit into the blast of icy air was enough to wake him up, and he had to do this again and again. Lindbergh forgot to check his course and failed to notice that the engine was running badly. He was losing control of his own reactions.

Just in time, Lindbergh reached the coast of Ireland. Seeing boats beneath him, he flew down to wave at them and the strain of being alone was broken. Lindbergh found that his concentration returned. In a few hours he had found his way to Paris, then he flew north to Le Bourget where he was due to land. Wild, cheering crowds greeted him, and a police escort fought to prevent Lindbergh and his plane from being crushed by the mob. Exhausted from his tense flight, he wanted only to sleep.

Lindbergh's epic flight started a new craze for flying long distances alone. In 1928 Bert Hinkler flew alone from London to Australia in record time. Two years later, Amy Johnson became the first woman to fly the same route solo, repairing her airplane several times after crash landings. Another British woman, the hon. Mrs. Bruce, flew alone around the world in 1930. In the eleven years after Alcock and Brown first crossed the Atlantic, almost every long-distance challenge had been conquered.

# Flying the Atlantic

Flying the Atlantic is no longer unusual. Many international airlines operate dozens of flights between the Americas and Europe every day. Passengers can travel by enormous Boeing 747 Jumbo jets, the supersonic Concorde service, or on a range of smaller aircraft.

Modern airports are very different from Lester's Field. Alcock and Brown bumped over uneven grass, but today's jets speed smoothly down paved runways. Passengers arrive at enormous terminal buildings, several hours before their flight departures. They check in at the flight desk and hand over their luggage to be weighed. While they wait for the call to board their plane, the passengers can amuse themselves in shops, bars, and restaurants.

Inside the aircraft the passengers can relax in comfortable chairs, and on long flights they can go to sleep. Meals are served, and often there are movies. The pilots sit in comfort on warm spacious flight decks and are not cramped in a cold, open cockpit like Alcock and Brown. Navigation is done with the help of electronic aids. Radar gives the pilots warning if any other planes are near. Direction-finding instruments follow the signals sent out by radio beacons placed on land and others fixed in satellites

**Below** *A photograph of Croydon Airport, near London, in 1932. This airport was one of the busiest in the world during the early days of aviation.*

**Above right** The Voyager, piloted by Rutan and Yeager, flew non-stop around the world in 1986.

**Above left** In the 1970s, the development of the Concorde, which is able to fly at supersonic speeds, changed our attitude toward flying across the Atlantic. It is now possible to fly from the United States to London and back during the space of a single day.

orbiting the Earth. Decoding the signals, a computer can pinpoint an airplane's exact position in seconds and give a precise course to the destination. An autopilot can take over the pilot's work during the flight.

On landing, the passengers move from the plane to a terminal building. They collect their luggage and pass through to the world outside. If they have arrived at London's Heathrow airport they may pass a statue of Alcock and Brown, the first people to fly non-stop across the Atlantic.

Although long-distance air travel is now an everyday occurrence, the pioneering spirit of Alcock and Brown lives on, and people invent new challenges all the time. In 1986 two Americans, Dick Rutan and Jeanna Yeager, made a non-stop flight right around the world. It took them nine days, in a specially designed aircraft. For the whole journey they shared a tiny cockpit only 0.6 m (2 ft) wide.

Seven years earlier, in 1979, a cyclist crossed the English Channel in a pedal-powered aircraft. Brian Allen pedaled non-stop for 2 hours and 49 minutes to cover the 36 km (22 mi) from Dover to Calais. At one point he was only inches above the waves, his aching muscles barely able to keep the pedals turning. When Blériot flew across the Channel in 1908, few people imagined how airplanes would develop.

# Glossary

**Aileron** The flap situated on the rear edge of an airplane's wing. The pilot uses the ailerons to control the angle of the plane's flight.

**Aerobatics** Difficult and dramatic maneuvers performed to demonstrate a pilot's skills. These may include very tight turns, loops, and spins. Such feats are often performed at air shows.

**Altitude** The measurement, taken from sea level, that shows the exact height of a plane.

**Air intake** The way in which air enters an engine to mix with the fuel. Without a steady supply of air, which contains oxygen, fuel cannot burn.

**Barnstorming** (of a pilot) Touring the country to give exhibitions of stunt flying, racing, etc.

**Biplane** An airplane that is designed with two sets of wings, one placed above the other.

**Cockpit** The pilot's cabin on an aircraft.

**Compass** An instrument that includes a magnetic needle. The needle points toward the magnetic north (situated near the North Pole). Such instruments are essential for navigation.

**Flying boat** An airplane designed to land on water. The fuselage is shaped like a boat, and instead of landing wheels, a flying boat has floats beneath each wing.

**Generator** A machine that is used to create electricity.

**Horizon** The line that, to the human eye, marks the point where the sky meets the sea or land.

**Monoplane** An airplane that is designed with only one set of wings.

**Navigation** The skill used to find the best route from one point to another.

**Parapet** The wall built at the edge of a high structure or building.

**Test pilot** A pilot who tests new airplanes to check that they perform successfully.

**Throttle** The accelerator, which controls the engine's speed.

**Wing struts** The poles, made of wood or metal, that are used to join together the two sets of wings on a biplane.

# Picture Acknowledgments

The publishers would like to thank the following for allowing their illustrations to be used in this book:

Chapel Studios 29 (top left); Mary Evans Picture Library 7 (top and bottom), 8 (top left, right and bottom), 9, 24 (bottom left), 25 (top); The Mansell Collection 22 (bottom), 23 (top), 26; Peter Newark's Military Pictures *frontispiece*; Topham 6; 18 (top), 23 (bottom), 24 (top and bottom right), 27 (top and bottom) 28, 29; Vickers plc 16, 17, 18 (bottom); Wayland Picture Library 4; Zefa 12, 22 (top). The cover illustration, portraying Alcock and Brown's transatlantic flight, is an oil painting by E. R. J. Moseling, a member of the Guild of Aviation Artists, entitled *Against the Elements*. All maps are provided by Peter Bull Art Studio.

# Finding out More

The best collection of early airplanes can be seen at the National Air and Space Museum in the Smithsonian Institution, Washington, D.C. On exhibit is the Wright brothers' 1903 *Flyer,* the first airplane to fly, and The *Spirit of St. Louis*, in which Charles Lindbergh made the first solo transatlantic flight from New York to Paris.

Perhaps you could try to build model gliders, like those the Wright brothers tested their ideas with. You can buy balsa wood at most modeling shops, and with this you can to experiment with your own aircraft designs.

# Books to Read

David Jefferies & Christopher Maynard, *The Aces: Pilots and Planes of World War I.* Franklin Watts, 1987

David Jefferies, *Epic Flights: Trailblazing Air Routes.* Franklin Watts, 1988

David Jefferies, *The First Flyers: Pioneers of Aviation.* Franklin Watts, 1988

Jason Hook, *The Wright Brothers.* Bookwright, 1989

Blythe Randolph, *Amelia Earhart.* Franklin Watts, 1987

Jom Robins, *The Story of Flight.* Warwick, 1987

# Index

ailerons **7, 30**
airfields
  Lester's Field **17-19**
  Quidi Vidi **14-19**
airports, modern **28**
Alcock, John
  Atlantic crossing **4, 20-23**
  in Canada before crossing **12-19**
  preparation for flight **16**
  on takeoff **18-19**
  training of **8-9**
  war service **9**
Allen, Brian **29**
Atlantic Ocean **4**
  challenge of crossing **8-9**
  first crossing east to west **25**
  first flight across **20-21**
  modern flights **28-9**
Australia, flights to **24, 27**

Blériot, Louis **6, 29**
Brooklands Racetrack **8**
Brown, Arthur Whitten
  Atlantic crossing **4, 20-23**
  in Canada before crossing **12-19**
  chosen as navigator **9**
  navigation skills **9**
  setting course **19**
  on takeoff **18-19**
  war service **9**
Bruce, Mrs. Victor **27**
Byrd, Richard **25**

Canada, flight from **4, 10**
  *see also* Newfoundland

clothing, for flight **11**
Cody, Samuel F. **6**

*Daily Mail* prize **8, 9, 12, 23**

English Channel, flight across **6, 29**

Farman, Henry **7**
Flight, the early development of **5-7**
*Flyer I* **5, 7**
flying boats **13, 30**
France
  Lindbergh's landing in **27**
  Wilbur Wright in **5, 6**

Handley Page team **8, 12-13, 17**
Hawker, Henry **12-16**
Hinkler, Bert **27**

Ireland **10**
  landing in **23**
  Lindbergh over **27**

Johnson, Amy **27**

Kerr, Admiral **12-13**
Kingsford-Smith, Charles **25**

Lindbergh, Charles **25, 26-7**

Martinsyde team **8, 12-14**
Morgan, Fairfax **14**

navigation **9, 19, 28-9, 30**
Newfoundland **10, 12-13**

Northcliffe, Lord Alfred **8**

Pacific Ocean **25**
passenger routes **25**

Raynham, Frederick **12-15, 17, 19**
Rutan, Dick **29**

Smith, Ross **24**
Sopwith team **8, 12-16**
South Africa, flight to **24**
*Spirit of St. Louis* **26**
Sunbeam **8**

Vickers team **8**
Vickers Vimy airplane
  Atlantic crossing **20-23**
  engines **10**
  *Daily Mail* prize **8**
  flight to Australia **24**
  flight to South Africa **24**
  landing in Ireland **23**
  preparation of **10-11**
  radio in **10, 14**
  reconstruction of **16-17**
  takeoff **18-19**
  wartime development of **7**

World War I
  Alcock and Brown in **9**
  and development of airplanes **7**
Wright brothers **5**

Yeager, Jeanna **29**